FASCINATION
MOUNTAIN LIVING

BRAUN

FASCINATION MOUNTAIN LIVING

ARCHITECTURE AND DESIGN

BRAUN CHRIS VAN UFFELEN

CONTENTS

10 HOUSE CAREZZA
monovolume architecture + design

16 AJISAI HOUSE
IDEE architects

22 BUČINA COTTAGE
ADR

28 WORKSHOP HOUSE
Tectum Arquitectura + Agustín Berzero

34 SELVA ALEGRE HOUSE
Lepannen Anker Arquitectura

40 CASA ROMAGNOLO
Wespi de Meuron Romeo architects
Studio D'Archittetura Concerpio

46 MOUNTAIN DUST
Mahesh Naik

52 L'ALIZÉ
Atelier Boom-Town

58 CASA ROCA
PPAA

64 WEST STOCKBRIDGE RESIDENCE
Resolution 4 Architecture

70 RESIDENCE HINTERKAISER
Bogenfeld Architektur

76 VILLA M
CRUU Architecture

82 HOUSE FP IN FELDKIRCH
Catharina Fineder Architektur

88 SKYHAVEN RESIDENCE
Blankpage Architects

94 RECTORY ST. BLASIEN
SPIECKER SAUER LAUER ARCHITEKTEN

100 ROOM WITH A VIEW
Martin Mostböck. ArchitectureInteriorDesign

106 A CHALET IN NENDAZ
Kündig & El Sadek

112 MAISON DE VACANCES K
counson architectes

CONTENTS

118
BARN HOUSE
Atelier Jörg Rügemer

124
MICHELBACH 1A
Michael Welle Architektur

130
HOUSE SCHALWYK
Drawbox Design Studio Architects

136
ROCKY MOUNTAIN HOUSE #1
Forma Architecture

142
HOUSE K
Architekt Torsten Herrmann

148
RIDGE 52 RESIDENCE
Ward | Blake Architects

154
HOUSE IM REBGÄRTLE
Aicher Architekten

160
NO FOOTPRINT WOODHOUSE
A-01 (A Company / A Foundation)

166
O' CASELLA
Atelier LAVIT

172
HOUSE BETWEEN THE MOUNTAINS
Gangoly & Kristiner Architekten

178
SAPIRE RESIDENCE
Abramson Architects

184
ZEIT. RAUM. WENG.
LP architektur

190
CHALET D
Lupo & Zuccarello Architekten

196
CAREZZA HOUSE
tara

202
MM HOUSE
BENJAMIN GOÑI ARQUITECTOS
CLARO + WESTENDARP ARQUITECTOS

208
THE THREE SUMMITS
NÓS architects

214
EL MONTAÑES
Gonzalo Iturriaga Arquitectos

Caspar Goar Wolf

Bridge and Gorges of Dala River in Leuekerbad, View towards the Mountain, c. 1774– 1777
Oil/canvas
82.5 cm × 54.2 cm
Valais Art Museum, Switzerland

Bridge and Gorges of Dala River in Leuekerbad, View towards the valley c. 1774–1777
Oil/canvas
82.5 cm × 54.2cm
Valais Art Museum, Switzerland

In the 1770s, a new motif emerged as the main subject of Classicist and Romantic painting: mountains. Caspar Goar Wolf was regarded as the forerunner of Alpine painting, and a pioneer who recorded mountains, gorges, and cliffs that were considered dangerous at the time.

PREFACE

If the fascination of Seaside Living is life on the edge of the elements, the fascination of Mountain Living is life amidst the elements. The remoteness and eternal majesty of the peaks, coupled with the diversity and power of the elements, have long attracted artists, particularly painters and writers. Since the classical era, these qualities have inspired a sense of *heroism* and *sublimity*, evoking the enduring presence of rocky eternity, the relentless forces of nature, the solitude of man, and the resilience of humanity. As early as the 17th century, this quality of the mountains was identified, particularly in the high mountains of Switzerland, during the Grand Tour, a journey undertaken by the bourgeoisie to explore the legacies of antiquity in Italy, especially by the English. It is therefore unsurprising that the first bookable group tour by Thomas Cook, the man who pioneered mass tourism, led to the Swiss Alps in 1863.

The allure of the mountains lies in the harmonious coexistence of the eternal and the chaotic, the tranquil and the tumultuous, which continues to draw builders and residents alike. The environment of rugged rocks and cliffs – evidence of powerful geological processes that have shaped the landscape over time – and the diverse flora and fauna that have adapted to this unique setting present an exceptional opportunity for construction and development. Consequently, these geographical conditions present a significant challenge in terms of construction in mountainous areas. The remoteness of construction sites leads to logistical obstacles in the transportation of building materials and machinery. This is also a key reason why local building materials and traditional techniques become attractive. Extreme snowfall, strong winds, icy temperatures, and sudden changes in weather, including unpredictable rainfall, can also have a significant impact on construction projects. These conditions place demands on materials, construction forms, or technical measures, such as the drainage of water from rainfall or melting snow. Furthermore, construction on mountains must contend with unique climatic conditions and frequently occurs in ecologically sensitive areas and natural landscapes. It is therefore essential to pay particular attention to the protection of the natural environment in every construction project. Building in mountainous areas necessitates a combination of technical expertise, innovative solutions, and a profound respect for the natural environment and the underlying geological conditions. By employing the appropriate strategies and modern technologies, as demonstrated in *Fascination Mountain Living,* it is possible to construct safe, functional, and sustainable buildings in harmony with nature, which also enhance the aesthetics of the surrounding area.

10

MONOVOLUME ARCHITECTURE + DESIGN

HOUSE CAREZZA

HOUSE CAREZZA

CAREZZA
ITALY

AREA
380 m²

YEAR
2023

PHOTOGRAPHY
Giovanni De Sandre
www.giovannidesandre.com

    Not far from Lake Carezza, in the Eggental valley, surrounded by lush larch forests and rugged peaks, lies House Carezza. The two new wooden houses translate the alpine architectural tradition of farmhouses into the present by combining materials such as wood and stone with modern technologies and reinterpreting the material separation between the upper and lower parts that is characteristic of this type of building. From above, one can see the asymmetrical roof geometry, which is reminiscent of the rough, fragmented materiality of rocks. Inside, the three floors are staggered so that the view of the panorama is guaranteed at all times. On the ground floor, each flat consists of an entrance area, the kitchen, the living room, and a wardrobe. On the upper floor, the large panoramic windows look directly onto the Dolomites. The building is certified with KlimaHouse A Nature.

A   Fir wood façade on a dolomite rock base draws a clear line
B   Two new houses united and seperated

13 HOUSE CAREZZA

CAREZZA
ITALY

D

E

F

C   South side opens up view of the Latemar Group
D   Living room and terrace
E   Fireplace combines alpine and modern elements
F   Bedroom with timeless atmosphere

15 HOUSE CAREZZA

CAREZZA
ITALY

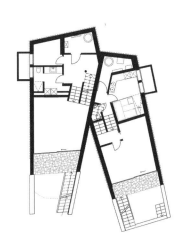
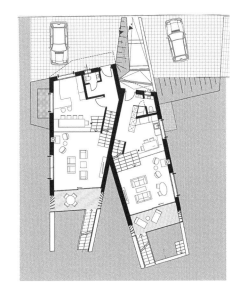
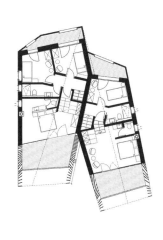

I

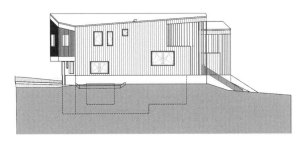

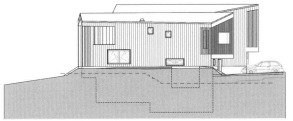

J

- G Wooden slats grant for privacy in the north
- H Glass façade facing the mountain on the south
- I Basement, ground and first floor plans
- J Sections

16

AJISAI
HOUSE

IDEE ARCHITECTS

17

AJISAI HOUSE

VĨNH PHÚC
VIETNAM

AREA
700 m²

YEAR
2021

PHOTOGRAPHY
Triệu Chiến

The house is situated on a steep mountain slope that provides a stunning view but was challenging in terms of access. With a land area of 1,000 square meters, the client desired an open, nature-oriented residence with a sense of privacy. The space should accommodate an extended family with five bedrooms and additional auxiliary spaces. The architects divided the property into two parts. The upper block is placed at the highest point, offering abundant natural light, ventilation, and panoramic views. The lower block includes a garage and auxiliary functions, serving as the primary access point from the front road. A slender elevator block connects this with the main house via a steel bridge, initiating a journey through the garden, swimming pool, front yard, and to the house. The main house is constructed with a steel frame, is symmetrical and allows cross ventilation.

A   Living room overlooking Tam Dao mountain range
B   Steel bridge above garden and swimming pool

19 AJISAI HOUSE

VĨNH PHÚC
VIETNAM

C   Tower volume with garage giving access to main volume

20

IDEE ARCHITECTS

D

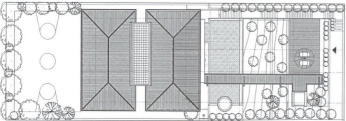

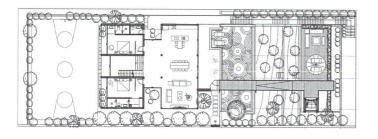

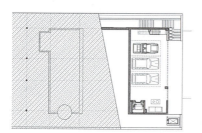

E

21 AJISAI HOUSE

VĨNH PHÚC
VIETNAM

D   Rear view with basketball field
E   Top view, first and ground floor plan
F   Bedroom with en-suite bath on second floor
G   Axis and central void define space in traditional Vietnamese architecture
H   Main house with steel frame, natural stone, and wood finish

22 BUČINA COTTAGE

ADR

23

BUČINA COTTAGE

HORNÍ MALÁ ÚPA
CZECH REPUBLIC

CLIENT
SKiMU Skiareal Malá Úpa

AREA
162 m²

YEAR
2023

PHOTOGRAPHY
BoysPlayNice
www.boysplaynice.com

The client's brief was to design a functional, compact building for the manager of a ski resort. The morphology of the floor plans asymmetrical cross derives from the traditional construction in the Krkonoše National Park area and the red paint is historically characteristic of wooden mountain buildings. Each arm of this cross-shaped building has a different function and offers a unique view. Notably, the dining area offers seating by a window with a view topped by the silhouette of Sněžka. At the intersection of the axes, there is a spiral staircase that winds around a chimney and offers a pleasant sitting area by the fireplace. The building is designed as a lightweight single-story wooden structure with a residential attic, resting on a concrete foundation slab that floats above the adjacent terrain in the summer, and levels with the snow cover in the winter.

A   Entrance to the red painted wooden building
B   Cross shaped volume from above

25 BUČINA COTTAGE

HORNÍ MALÁ ÚPA
CZECH REPUBLIC

C   Terrace on south side hovering on concrete plinth above the snow

27 BUČINA COTTAGE

HORNÍ MALÁ ÚPA
CZECH REPUBLIC

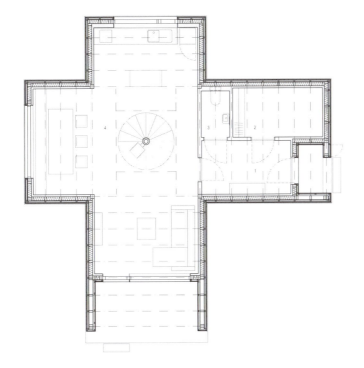
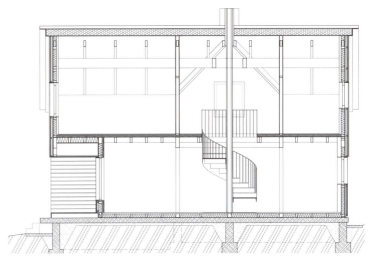
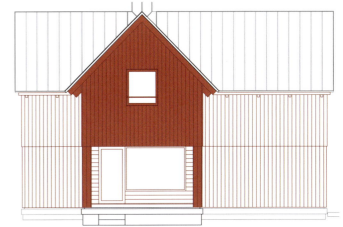

G H

D   Large window with view to the mountain side
E   Spiral staircase on ground floor
F   Spiral staircase in upper floor
G   Ground floor plan
H   North-south section and north elevation

28

WORKSHOP HOUSE

TECTUM ARQUITECTURA + AGUSTÍN BERZERO

29 WORKSHOP HOUSE

CÓRDOBA
ARGENTINA

AREA
54 m²
YEAR
2022
PHOTOGRAPHY
Federico Cairoli
www.federicocairoli.com

This project is located in Córdoba, on an almost 45-degree slope. The design balances contrasts, with the lower section built for structural support using heavier materials, while the upper part is lighter in construction. The house opens up to take in views and natural light, while also including more enclosed areas for quiet contemplation. The entry is via the roof, beneath the highest point on the lot, connected to the house by a bridge. The space is characterized by varied proportions, shifting ceiling heights, and a dynamic interplay of openings and enclosures that frame or obscure the surrounding landscape. Inside, the house is entirely clad in warm wood, contrasting with the rugged exterior. Reinforced concrete defines the structure, shapes the spaces, and establishes a connection with both, the earth and the sky. This house offers a retreat from the outside world, integrating harmoniously with the natural topography.

A   Celebrating the encompassing landscape
B   View of the monolithic structure

30

TECTUM ARQUITECTURA + AGUSTÍN BERZERO

C   Front view without alternations to topography
D   Bridge
E   Roof acces
F   Versatile space hovering treetops

31 WORKSHOP HOUSE

CÓRDOBA
ARGENTINA

E

F

TECTUM ARQUITECTURA + AGUSTÍN BERZERO

33 WORKSHOP HOUSE

CÓRDOBA
ARGENTINA

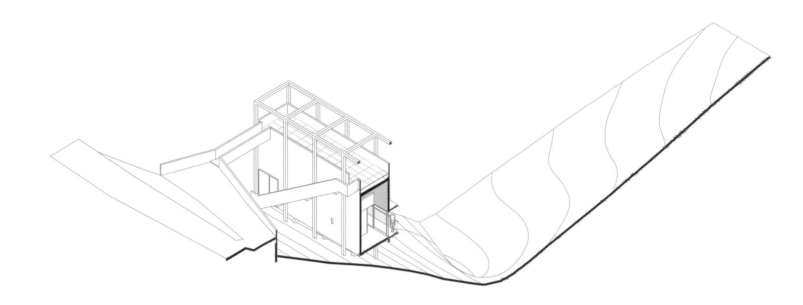

J

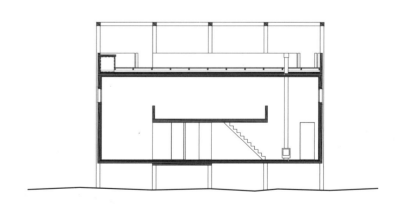

G Wooden cladding
H Work space
I Interior scales
J Axonometric section
K Longitudinal plan

K

34

LEPANNEN ANKER ARQUITECTURA

SELVA ALEGRE HOUSE

35 SELVA ALEGRE HOUSE

SANGOLQUI
ECUADOR

INTERIOR DESIGN
Insólito
LANDSCAPE DESIGN
Mónica Bodenhorst
AREA
450 m²
YEAR
2020
PHOTOGRAPHY
BICUBIK (A–C, E)
bicubik.photo
JAG STUDIO (D, F)
jagstudio.ec

Selva Alegre was designed to draw inspiration from its natural surroundings, particularly the Andes Mountains of Ecuador. The design strategy prioritized an open ground floor with clear divisions, evoking the layout of a traditional hacienda house but with a modern approach. The former central patio was transformed into a water feature that divides and connects social and private spaces via an actual bridge. The concept uses traditional materials in a modern way, creating a sense of lightness and airiness. By combining elements with varied heights and openings, the mountain was connected visually. A flowing roof gracefully protects interior spaces. Overhead skylights flood the pool and main spaces with light and optimize air flow and temperature year-round. The design blends the building with the natural landscape, creating a tranquil and immersive experience for its inhabitants.

A View of the curved roof
B Angles of the façade

LEPANNEN ANKER ARQUITECTURA

37 SELVA ALEGRE HOUSE

SANGOLQUI
ECUADOR

C   Living area with view of transparency in the roof

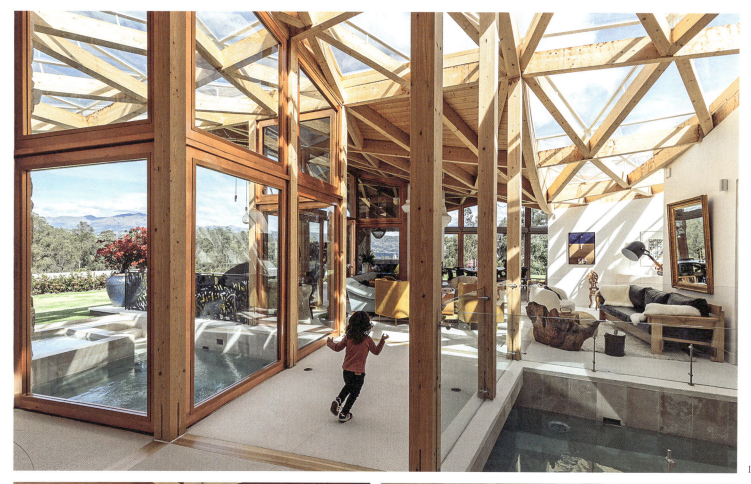

D

E F

39 SELVA ALEGRE HOUSE

SANGOLQUI
ECUADOR

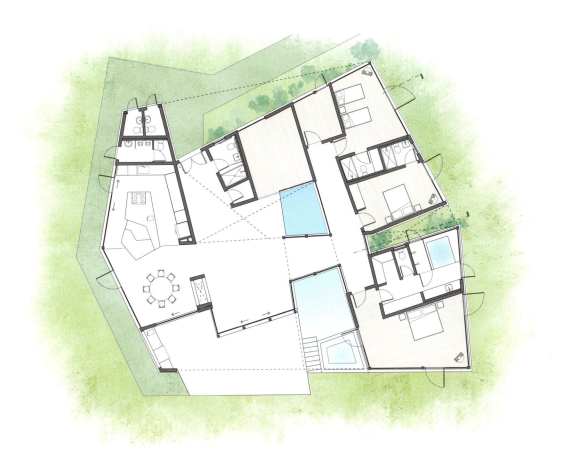

D   Pool connecting interior and exterior
E   Close-up pool and bridge
F   Master bathroom with opening to the outdoors
G   Plan
H   Integrated wooden structural system

40

WESPI DE MEURON ROMEO ARCHITECTS
STUDIO D'ARCHITETTURA CONCEPRIO

CASA ROMAGNOLO

41 CASA ROMAGNOLO

MAROLTA
SWITZERLAND

AREA
330 m²

YEAR
2024

PHOTOGRAPHY
Giacomo Albo
www.finearc.it

As the design and architecture of the Casa Romagnolo were still in good original state, corrections were largely limited to the access and entrance situation and the north-facing extension for the bathrooms. While the richly decorated main façade was still intact, a relocation of the village street led to a missing connection, which was restored by a new flat sloping path. This also provides access to the vaulted cellar. At the rear, a new volume for the bathrooms was added to the main floor, which here appears as a low rural building without the basement. The extension has a clear, contemporary architectural design, but the dry stone masonry also echoes the texture of the historic slate roof of Casa Romagnolo. Inside, the transition to the bathrooms with roof glazing already appears like an outdoor space and behind the bathrooms there are corresponding walled courtyards.

A Northern extension with dry stone masonry like the neighboring building
B Central corridor between the two bathrooms and courtyards

C

43 CASA ROMAGNOLO

MAROLTA
SWITZERLAND

D

E

F

C   Front façade with new path leading up to the cellar
D   Dining table in the restored room
E   New kitchen opposite to the dining table
F   Sliding Corten steel door next to kitchen and dining

WESPI DE MEURON ROMEO ARCHITECTS
STUDIO D'ARCHITETTURA CONCEPRIO

45 CASA ROMAGNOLO

MAROLTA
SWITZERLAND

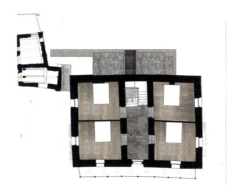

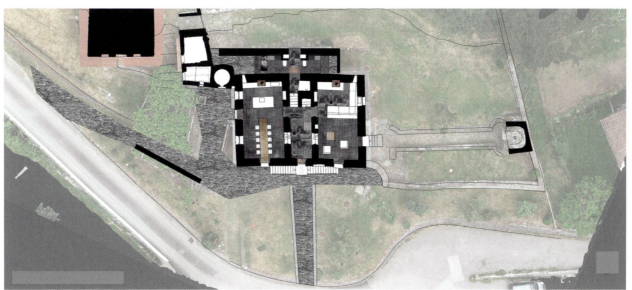

K

G   New western bathroom with tub
H   New eastern bathroom with smaller courtyard
I   Corridor facing north
J   Corridor with stairs to the historical building
K   Ground and first floor plan
L   Section

L

46

MOUNTAIN DUST

MAHESH NAIK

47 MOUNTAIN DUST

PANVEL
INDIA

CLIENT
Alreja

AREA
7,295 m²

YEAR
2023

PHOTOGRAPHY
Mahesh Naik (A–C, F)
Omkar Jagdale and Musaib (E)

This house is situated within the Indian state of Maharashtra. The concept for the house was to integrate three key elements: the imposing mountain, the sunrise, and the moon. This resulted in the creation of a sacred knot, a triskelion geometry, which became the key design element of the house. The color scheme was also developed in accordance with the triskelion geometry, as the primary colors are beige, red, and black. This approach allows the house to have a larger surface area, providing a comprehensive 360-degree view of the surrounding mountains. The external appearance of the house is a direct consequence of this process. In order to enhance the green coverage of the property, over 2,000 trees were planted over a period of three years. However, the landscape surrounding Mountain Dust has been maintained in a natural state, characterised by a random and raw quality.

A   Front view of the building
B   Side view

49 MOUNTAIN DUST

PANVEL
INDIA

C   Buildung at dusk

MAHESH NAIK

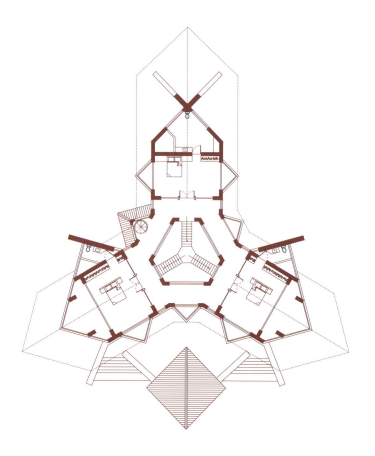
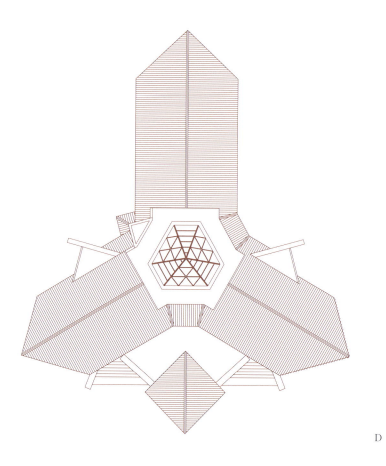
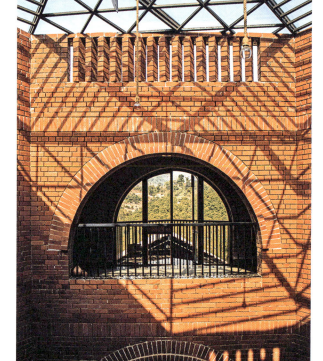

D   Plans, first floor and roof
E   Insight from the view on the stairs
F   Staircases in the center

52

L'ALIZÉ

ATELIER BOOM-TOWN

53 L'ALIZÉ

QUEBEC
CANADA

AREA
328 m²

YEAR
2023

PHOTOGRAPHY
Raphaël Thibodeau

This residence is on a peak in Wentworth-Nord, Canada. The Alizé house sits on a hillside and is designed to withstand wind and weather. Its two main volumes intersect at a central point, which is the residence's anchor. The roofs run north to south. The house has a garage, a carport, a laundry room, and a large terrace. From east to west, the living room, kitchen, dining room, study, and bedroom are situated beneath a long, low-pitched roof. While the east-facing living room looks out over the estate and Lake Notre-Dame, the south facing façade opens to the surroundings. Roof projections regulate solar gain in summer and provide weatherproof outdoor space. The monochromatic exterior is achieved through the use of wood, steel, black aluminum windows, and an exposed concrete wall, allowing the surroundings to stand out. Inside, polished concrete floors store and diffuse heat.

A Front view
B South façade

55 L'ALIZÉ

QUEBEC
CANADA

D

E

F

C Terrace
D Kitchen and hallway
E Bathroom
F Living room

ATELIER BOOM-TOWN

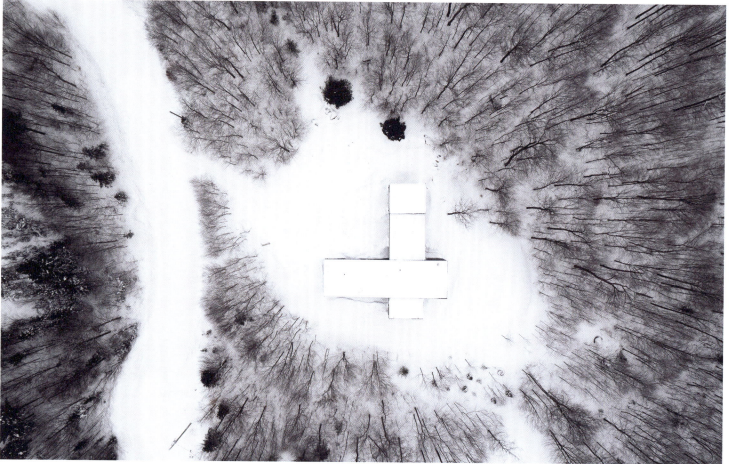

G

H

G   Aerial view
H   View from above
I   First floor plan
J   Ground floor plan

57 L'ALIZÉ

QUBEC
CANADA

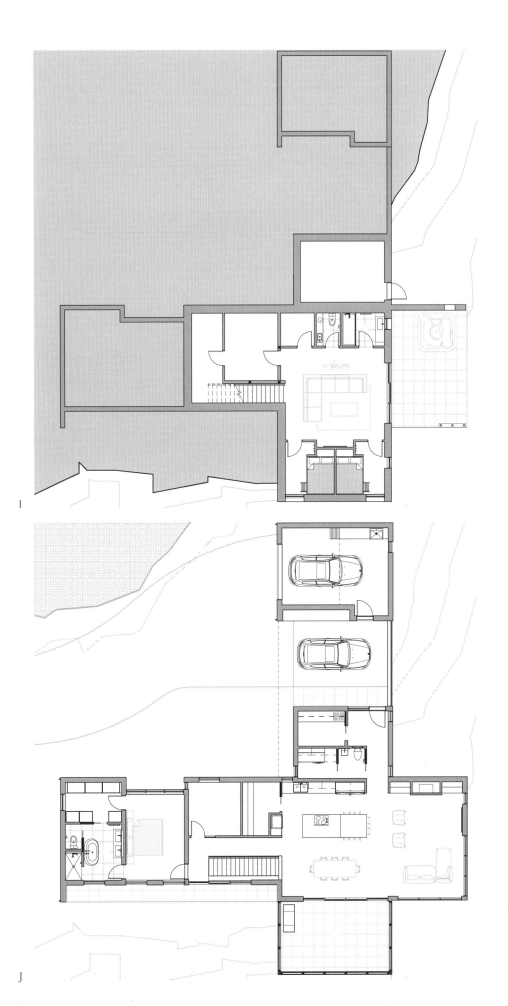

58

CASA ROCA

PPAA

59

CASA ROCA

YOSEMITE LAKES
CA, USA

CLIENT
Juan Pablo Santillan and
Tania Alvarado

AREA
91.87 m²

YEAR
2023

PHOTOGRAPHY
Rafael Gamo
www.rafaelgamo.com

Casa Roca is located in Yosemite Lakes, overlooking the national park. This house was designed to blend seamlessly into the landscape. The house layout faces impressive views. This was achieved by placing windows that allow lots of light while showing the surroundings, creating a strong link between residents and nature; as well as featuring an outdoor area for residents to enjoy the natural environment. The sloping roof mirrors the angle of the mountain and the wood façade blends the house into its surroundings. The warm interior fosters a cozy atmosphere. Additionally, stone and concrete create a raw, natural aesthetic with exposed floors. Three large rocks were integrated into the entrance, establishing a connection with the rocky landscape. Casa Roca was designed to offer visual transparency, allowing residents to feel immersed in nature.

A   North façade
B   Panoramic views from
    inside the house

61 CASA ROCA

YOSEMITE LAKES
CA, USA

C Integrated into the environment

63 CASA ROCA

YOSEMITE LAKES
CA, USA

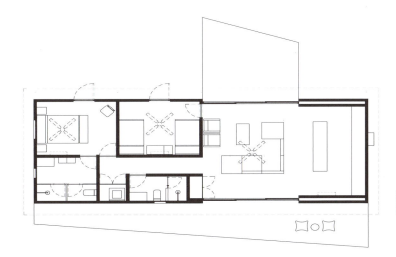
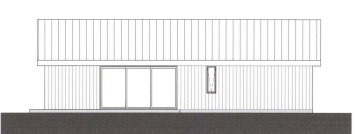

F G

D West façade
E Sketch
F Floor plan
G Main façade
H Roof aligning with slope of the mountain

H

64

RESOLUTION: 4 ARCHITECTURE

WEST STOCKBRIDGE RESIDENCE

65 WEST STOCKBRIDGE RESIDENCE

WEST STOCKBRIDGE
MA, USA

LANDSCAPE DESIGN
Webster Landscape

AREA
262 m²

YEAR
2020

PHOTOGRAPHY
Gavin Preuss/ Home and Property Photography LLC
homeandpropertyphotography.com

This modern modular home serves as a country retreat in the Berkshires, MA. Capitalizing on the nature of modular construction, the floor plan is broken into a series of volumes that slip into the landscape, providing opportunities for a courtyard deck, private and varied views, and more glazing on the façade. The slipping nature of the plan works with the sloping site, allowing some volumes to feel rooted in the hillside while others project out over the meadow. From a winding country road, the drive terminates at a covered carport that offers mountain views upon arrival through the foyer. The open living space features floor-to-ceiling glass, allowing the stunning landscape to take center stage. At one end of the home, two guest suites feature Murphy beds, allowing the rooms to double as offices. Opposite, a media room and library offer more mountain views and lead to a primary suite beyond, flooded with natural light.

A View through living space
B View from the hillside

B

RESOLUTION: 4 ARCHITECTURE

C   Merging with the hill
D   Built-in desks allow guest bedrooms to function as offices
E   Open living space
F   Views from the bathroom

67 WEST STOCKBRIDGE RESIDENCE — WEST STOCKBRIDGE, MA, USA

E

F

RESOLUTION 4: ARCHITECTURE

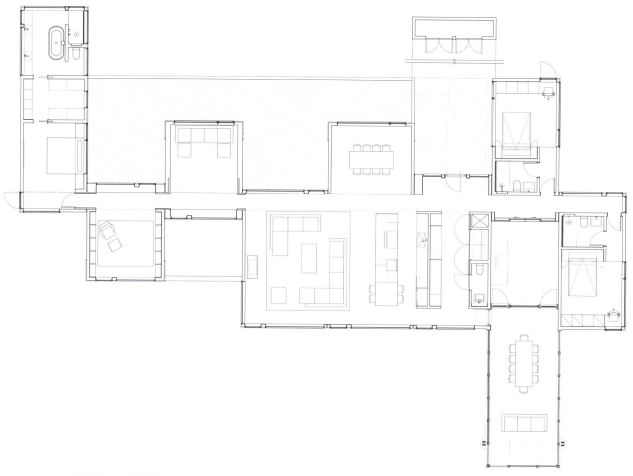

G   Floor plan
H   Pimary bedroom
I   Mountain views
J   Foyer

69 WEST STOCKBRIDGE RESIDENCE

WEST STOCKBRIDGE
MA, USA

70

BOGENFELD ARCHITEKTUR

RESIDENCE HINTERKAISER

71

RESIDENCE HINTERKAISER

ST JOHANN
AUSTRIA

AREA
309 m²
YEAR
2019
PHOTOGRAPHY
David Schreyer
www.schreyerdavid.com

This is a residential property located in St. Johann in Tyrol. The design idea was to create a form that would make passers-by think of a boulder fallen from the mountain and fitting harmoniously into the surroundings. Both, the floor plan and the materials used, the sharp edges and the striking pitched roof are based on this idea. The building was constructed in accordance with Tyrolean building regulations and is a solid construction with a perforated façade and larch windows. Additionally, a small-scale panel façade was constructed using Eternit rhomboids. The residence features a partial basement and is constructed on a plinth. Located on a split level, the entrance, which is at ground level serves as a checkroom but also as a spacious storage area. The house features shop-window-like openings that provide views of the greenery and a spacious, open central staircase leading up to the upper floor.

A   Front view
B   Street view

A

B

73 RESIDENCE HINTERKAISER

ST JOHANN
AUSTRIA

C   Outside view with mountains

75 RESIDENCE HINTERKAISER

ST JOHANN
AUSTRIA

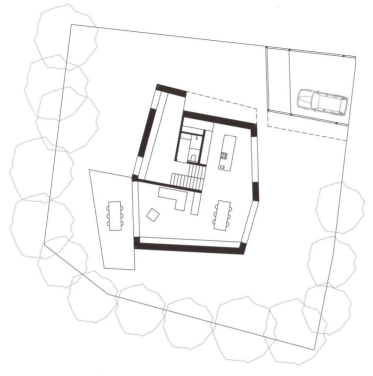
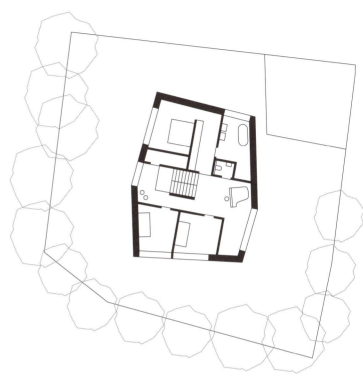

F G

D   Stairs to the rooms
    upstairs
E   Reception room
F   Ground floor plan
G   First floor plan
H   Nook

H

76 VILLA M

CRUU ARCHITECTURE

77

VILLA M

GORTIPOHL
AUSTRIA

CLIENT
m.properties
AREA
500 m²
YEAR
2022
PHOTOGRAPHY
Markus Mehwald
www.mehwald.net

In this building, two houses extend over the three staggered volumes of the stories, each of which has an individual modern design. The base, which is pushed into the slope, accommodates the two wellness areas and provides ground-level access to the spacious terrace and garden. The recessed living floor is generously glazed with a view of the Montafon valley. This floor is open and spacious, with large windows, an open kitchen, a dinning area, and a wood-burning in the living room. All stories are connected by an open staircase seperatly for each house. The bedrooms are located in the dark, floating structure. The different balcony and terrace levels also reflect different qualities of living. In front of the wellness area, one sits on the green meadow to the south with a view of the adjacent stream to the west; on ground floor a south-facing terrace offers views of the mountain Garfrescha.

A South side with wellness, living and bedroom story
B Dinning area with corner view of the Montafon

C

D

79 VILLA M

GORTIPOHL
AUSTRIA

C   Building with shared pool
D   Terrace and kitchen on the south side
E   Pool looking into nature

F

G

81 VILLA M

GORTIPOHL
AUSTRIA

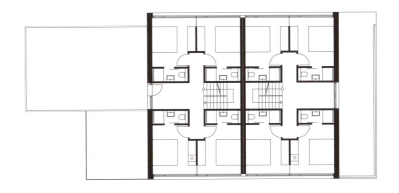

H

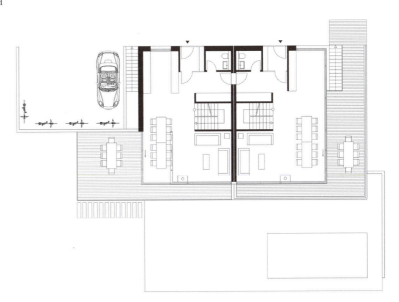

I

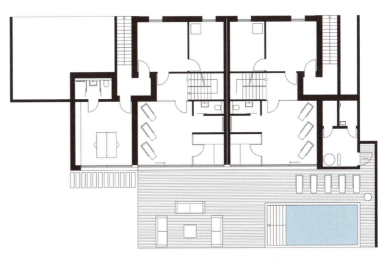

F Large windows providing plenty of light
G Dining area with fireplace
H First floor plan
I Ground floor plan
J Basement floor plan

J

82

CATHARINA FINEDER ARCHITEKTUR

HOUSE FP IN FELDKIRCH

83 HOUSE FP IN FELDKIRCH

FELDKIRCH
AUSTRIA

AREA
247.3 m²

YEAR
2019

PHOTOGRAPHY
Petra Rainer

The architect erected the building —which appears small from the outside but is extremely spacious on the inside — on a hillside plot on the Ardetzenberg with a 30 percent incline high above Feldkirch. With its light gray exterior plaster, gray aluminum frame, and very flat pitched roof in gray stainless steel, it blends in unpretentiously with the surrounding buildings. Inside, a retaining wall divides the floor space: from the entrance, one reaches the family table via the angled kitchen, which is already part of the spacious living room. From here, floor-to-ceiling glazing opens up the view over Feldkirch to the tops of the mountains Hohe Köpfe and Gurtisspitze. The sustainability concept includes a ventilation system with heat recovery, photovoltaics, a heat pump, and the use of predominantly HFC-free insulation materials.

A   A volume appears very small from the front but shows its actual size from the side
B   Terrace above Feldkirch

85 HOUSE FP IN FELDKIRCH

FELDKIRCH
AUSTRIA

C Entrance and kitchen separated by reataining wall from dining and living room

87 HOUSE FP IN FELDKIRCH

FELDKIRCH
AUSTRIA

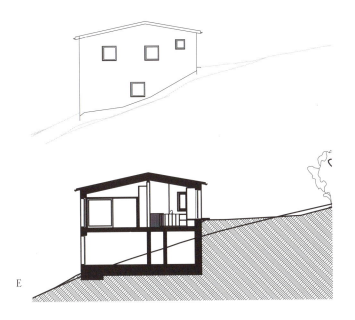
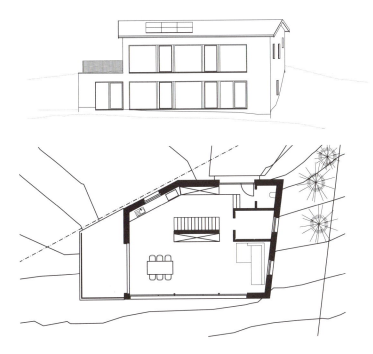

D   House FP above the valley looking to the Schattenburg Museum
E   Elevations, section and upper floor plan
F   Entrance
G   Angled kitchen and stairs to the lower level next to reatining wall

88

BLANKPAGE ARCHITECTS

SKYHAVEN RESIDENCE

89

SKYHAVEN RESIDENCE

GHOUMA
LEBANON

AREA
740 m²

YEAR
2023

PHOTOGRAPHY
Wissam Chaaya
www.wissamchaaya.com

Located on a spectacular hilltop in the Batroun region in Lebanon, this site overlooks a lush green valley with views to the sea. The project consists of two houses within one envelope: one house for the client and another for his parents. Given the topography and landscape context, the house is conceived as a balcony or belvedere in nature. The house's arched shape embraces the panorama. To reduce the impact of the excavation and retaining walls on such a steep site, the project consists of two floors supported by concrete corbels. The lower slab houses the bedrooms of both houses along with a meditation room referencing Japanese architecture and having a raised wooden platform surrounded by greenery on three sides. In addition, the living areas and open kitchens, fully glazed, enjoy unobstructed views. Sliding aluminum panels enhance the feeling of living on a balcony.

A   View towards the sea
B   Top view of the house

BLANKPAGE ARCHITECTS

C

D

C   Balcony in nature
D   Access ramp
E   Meditation room
F   Living area

91 SKYHAVEN RESIDENCE

GHOUMA
LEBANON

E

F

93 SKYHAVEN RESIDENCE

GHOUMA
LEBANON

I   J

G   Roof bridge connecting pool deck
H   Night aerial view
I   Ground floor plan
J   First floor plan

RECTORY ST. BLASIEN

94

SPIECKER SAUTTER LAUER ARCHITEKTEN

95 RECTORY ST. BLASIEN

ST. BLASIEN
GERMANY

LANDSCAPE ARCHITECTS
Krause Landschaftsarchitektur

CLIENT
Evangelische Christus-gemeinde St. Blasien

AREA
375 m²

YEAR
2021

PHOTOGRAPHY
Manfred Sautter (A, C)
Yohan Zerdoun (B, D–G)
www.yohanzerdoun.com

This new rectory in St. Blasien was built on a hillside above the town center. It serves as a replacement for the historic rectory on the opposite side of the valley, which was too large and therefore no longer economically viable. In addition to functionality, integration into the surroundings and the appearance of the building, ecological and sustainable construction methods were very important to the client. It was therefore important to plan a building that – thanks to its compactness and appropriate insulation standards – is highly efficient in operation. The structure of the building follows that of a traditional Black Forest House: The hillside floor with the office area consists of a solid double-shell concrete construction with core insulation. The actual rectory above is constructed almost exclusively from wood. This ensures a balanced indoor climate, and it conveys an impression of warmth and comfort.

A Outside perspective
B View into the valley

SPIECKER SAUTTER LAUER ARCHITEKTEN

97 RECTORY ST. BLASIEN

ST. BLASIEN
GERMANY

C   Outside perspective showing concrete and shingles

SPIECKER SAUTTER LAUER ARCHITEKTEN

99 RECTORY ST. BLASIEN

ST. BLASIEN
GERMANY

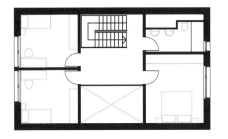

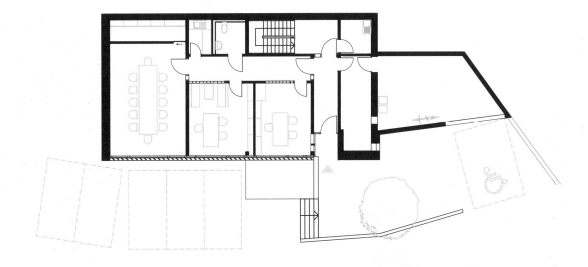

H

D View across the dining area
E Living area
F Corridor to the rectory
G Gallery to the bedroom floor
H First floor, ground floor, and hillside floor plan

100 ROOM WITH A VIEW

MARTIN MOSTBÖCK. ARCHITECTUREINTERIORSDESIGN

101 ROOM WITH A VIEW

FORCHTENSTEIN
AUSTRIA

AREA
198 m²

YEAR
2021

PHOTOGRAPHY
Nathan Murrell
www.nathanmurrellphotos.com

This house is located on the highest still buildable plot in a small community in northern Burgenland. It is located on the neighboring hill within sight of the region's famous medieval castle and is bordered by forests. The two-part structure is oriented east-west with a mountain view to the west and a valley view to the east. A platform with two conical volumes is created on the base, the entrance and the storage area. The west-facing volume stretches along the vertical axis to open up to the evening sun. The east-facing volume stretches along the vertical and horizontal axes, creating a beautiful view of the valley. Both volumes merge into one whole. The focus is on the kitchen with one side being equipped with a spacious dining area with a large terrace in front and an integrated whirlpool. On the other side of the kitchen, facing west, the recreation and lounge zone offers relaxation in the evening.

A   Furnished terrace with jacuzzi at night
B   South-facing terrace and façade with integrated lighting

MARTIN MOSTBÖCK. ARCHITECTUREINTERIORSDESIGN

C D

C Kitchen/living room view
D Bathroom
E View from the forest

MARTIN MOSTBÖCK. ARCHITECTUREINTERIORSDESIGN

F

G

F   South-facing terrace with side entrance
G   Facade detail
H   Cross section
I   First Floor

105 ROOM WITH A VIEW

FORCHTENSTEIN
AUSTRIA

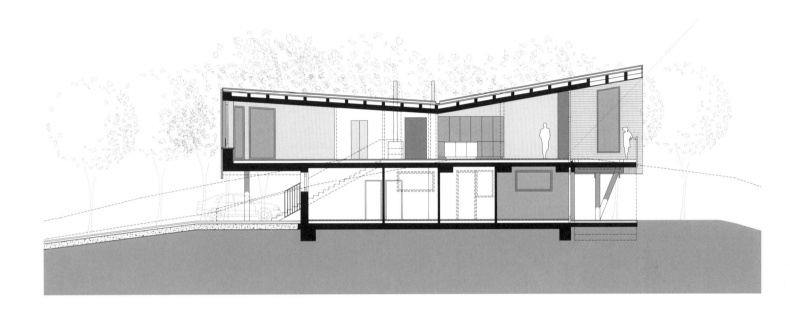

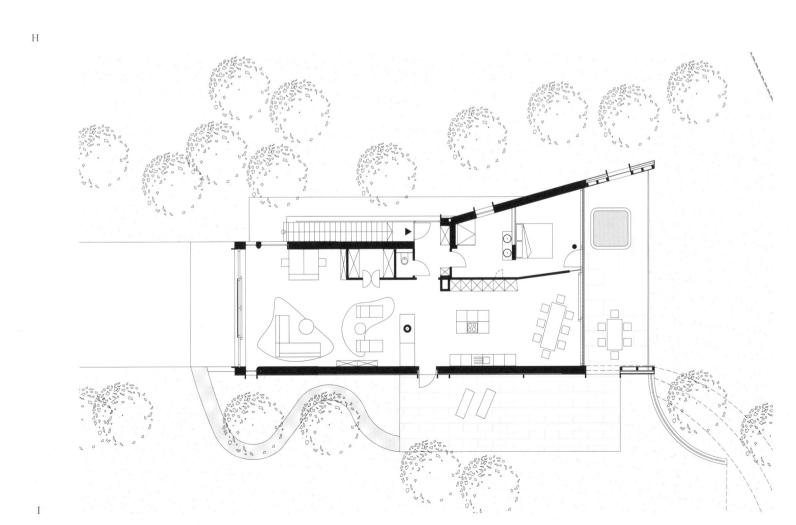

106
A CHALET IN NENDAZ

KÜNDIG & EL SADEK

107 A CHALET IN NENDAZ

NENDAZ
SWITZERLAND

AREA
200 m²

YEAR
2023

PHOTOGRAPHY
Kündig & El Sadek GmbH

Located on the outskirts of the village of Sornard – part of Nendaz –, the chalet, originally owned by the clients' parents, was renovated to meet the needs of the young family. It was also important to reconnect the house to the neighborhood and reorient it to the breathtaking views of the Alps. One main feature of the renovation is the addition of a new floor to the existing ground floor. The new roof, reversed from the original ridge, blends in harmoniously with its surroundings and optimizes the interior space. The façade reinterprets familiar barns of the region and the ground floor has been carefully preserved. Standing out for its self-build approach, the family, including two generations, carried out much of the dismantling and interior work. Details were designed with an emphasis on simplicity of execution to support this process, and a priorization of natural and locally sourced materials.

A   West façade and the alps
B   Southern façade

C Simple and warm interior
D Living space
E Window protected by the façade
F Window details

109 A CHALET IN NENDAZ

NENDAZ
SWITZERLAND

E

F

G   Chalet blending with its environment
H   Façade with vegetation
I   Ground floor plan
J   First floor plan
K   Longitudinal section

A CHALET IN NENDAZ

NENDAZ
SWITZERLAND

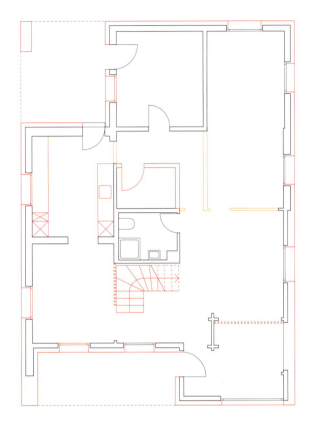 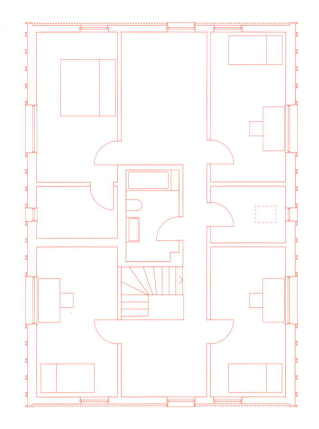

I J

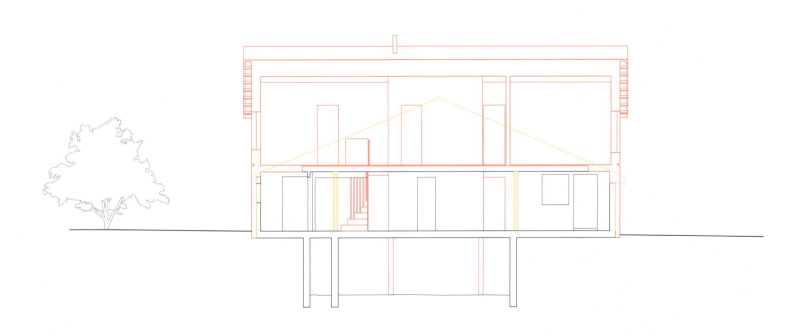

K

112

COUNSON ARCHITECTES

MAISON DE VACANCES K

113 MAISON DE VACANCES K

LES DIABLERETS
SWITZERLAND

AREA
160 m²

YEAR
2019

PHOTOGRAPHY
Leo Fabrizio

This residence is situated in a forest above the village of Les Diablerets, Switzerland. The new construction is on the site of an existing 1960s chalet that was outdated. The architectural style is inspired by traditional alpine building techniques. The Maison de Vacances K has two levels on a partially buried base. The first floor comprises the main living area and a loggia with panoramic views of the Vaud Alps. The second floor offers four bedrooms, two of which face north and the other two south. A checkroom, ski room and technical rooms can be accessed from the ground floor. The entire chalet is constructed exclusively of wood, including the black-stained FSC spruce framing and wood-wool insulation. The highly insulated envelope significantly reduces energy losses and is equipped with a heat pump that is fed by geothermal wells and solar panels.

A   Outside view
B   Kitchen

115 MAISON DE VACANCES K

LES DIABLERETS
SWITZERLAND

C View into the first floor
D Close-up stairs
E Entrance

D E

COUNSON ARCHITECTES

F   Panoramic view through the loggia
G   Loggia
H   Floor plans
I   Section

117 MAISON DE VACANCES K

LES DIABLERETS
SWITZERLAND

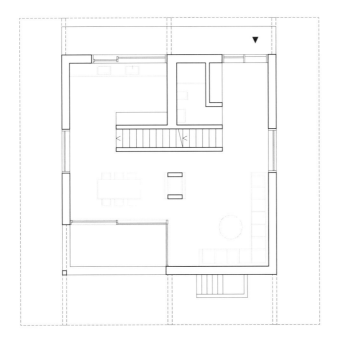
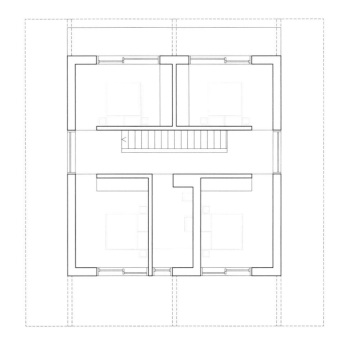

H

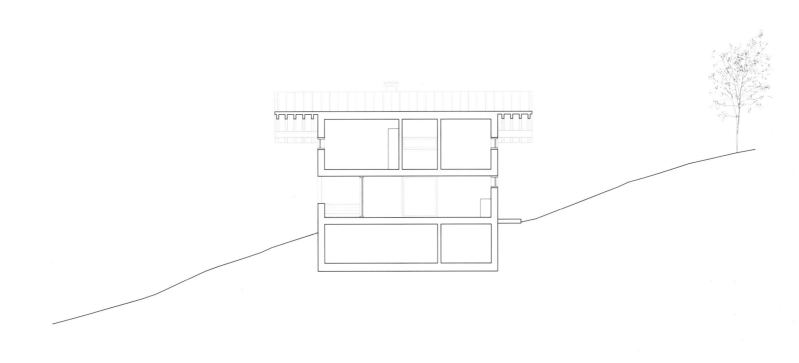

I

118

BARN
HAUS

ATELIER JÖRG RÜGEMER

119

BARN HAUS

HOLLADAY
UT, USA

CLIENT
Manuela and Lazarre Ogden
AREA
350 m²
YEAR
2020
PHOTOGRAPHY
Paul Richer
www.richerimages.com

    The Barn Haus is a zero-energy home that makes a significant contribution to sustainable housing in the southwestern United States. It is located at 1,650 meters in the western foothills of the Rocky Mountains and offers a fascinating view over the Salt Lake City metropolitan region. The Barn Haus has a design that combines sustainability, resilience, and efficiency in a strong concept and also takes an abstract approach of traditional Southwest barns. The Utah Contemporegional Style, coined by the architect, represents a modern interpretation of regional building elements. The minimalist house reflects the simplicity, functionality, and expressiveness of agricultural architecture, avoiding the decorative overdesign common to the region. The result balances tradition and modernity that makes the Barn Haus a role model for sustainable building.

A   House in the evening light
B   Overview from the south

121 BARN HAUS

HOLLADAY
UT, USA

C   South façade reinterprates regional buliding style

D

E F

123 BARN HAUS

HOLLADAY
UT, USA

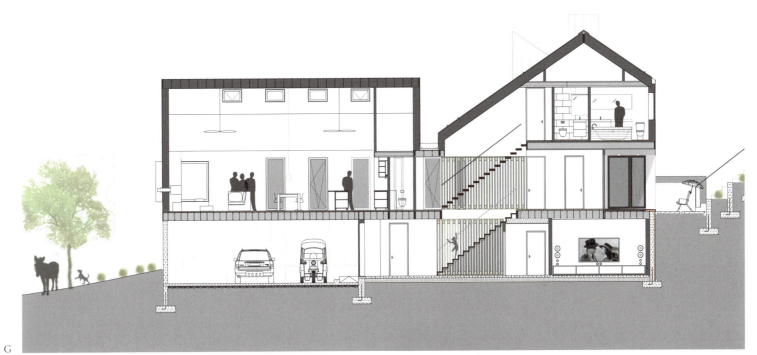

D   Garden terrace in the afternoon light
E   Downstairs bathroom
F   Children's room
G   Longitudinal section
H   Hallway

124

MICHAEL WELLE ARCHITEKTUR

MICHELBACH 1A

125

MICHELBACH IA

NORDRACH
GERMANY

AREA
481 m²

YEAR
2023

PHOTOGRAPHY
Jürgen Pollak & Patrick Möhrle

Michael Welle Architektur built this residential building on the ascent of the village of Nordarch into the Black Forest, which initially adapted to the terrain like a spur before developing into a prototypical gabled façade on the valley side after a kink in the volume. The structure follows the historical model of a typical Kinzigtäler House with a solid base storey and a timber construction for the upper storeys. Living and working take place under one roof. Typical regional materials and techniques create a connection to the region and the landscape. The residents wanted a pollutant-free building with the smallest possible ecological footprint. For this reason, the load-bearing structure, apart from the basement in contact with the ground, was made of wood. The walls are insulated with straw and equipped with a clay wall heating system.

A   Building on the spur-shaped plot
B   Traditional mix of materials with a view of Rhine valley

A B

MICHAEL WELLE ARCHITEKTUR

C   Staircase leading to corridor above the kitchen
D   Bathroom with a view
E   Kitchen in front of the staircase
F   Dining table in the kinking spur roof level

127 MICHELBACH IA

NORDRACH
GERMANY

E

F

129 MICHELBACH IA

NORDRACH
GERMANY

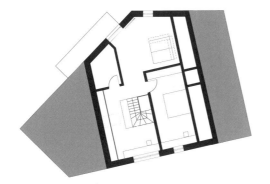
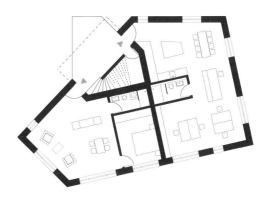
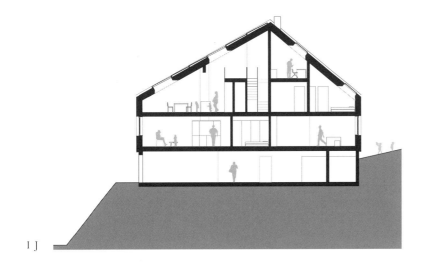
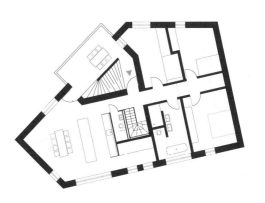

G   Balcony with a panoramic view
H   Michelbach IA opening up to the landscape
I   Second and first floor plan
J   Section and ground floor plan

130

DRAWBOX DESIGN STUDIO ARCHITECTS

HOUSE SCHALKWYK

131

HOUSE SCHALKWYK

BRONBERG MOUNTAIN
SOUTH AFRICA

CLIENT
Neil & Tonja Schalkwyk

AREA
200 m²

YEAR
2019

PHOTOGRAPHY
Natasha Dawjee Laurent
www.papercutphotography.com

The project connects an existing residence with an outbuilding used for entertainment on the southern slope of Bronberg Mountain in Pretoria, South Africa. Previously linked by a timber walkway through a forest and past a waterfall, the new design features a suspended glazed walkway that weaves through the forest, enhancing the natural experience. An elevated platform offers unique views, while a bedroom nestled in the forest provides a serene morning light experience. The extension of the outbuilding includes a play area, dining space, and lounge. To minimize site disturbance, the steel structure is suspended and supported only where necessary, integrating endangered trees as focal points. The design employs an exoskeleton of structural steel sections to blend with the forest and glazing to reflect its density. The building's form adapts to the site's contours and tree positions.

A   Dining on the elevated platform
B   Outbuilding with wooden deck

A
B

DRAWBOX DESIGN STUDIO ARCHITECTS

C

D

C Glazed walkway weaves through the forest
D Inside the walkway
E Dining from outside

F

G

135 HOUSE SCHALKWYK

BRONBERG MOUNTAIN
SOUTH AFRICA

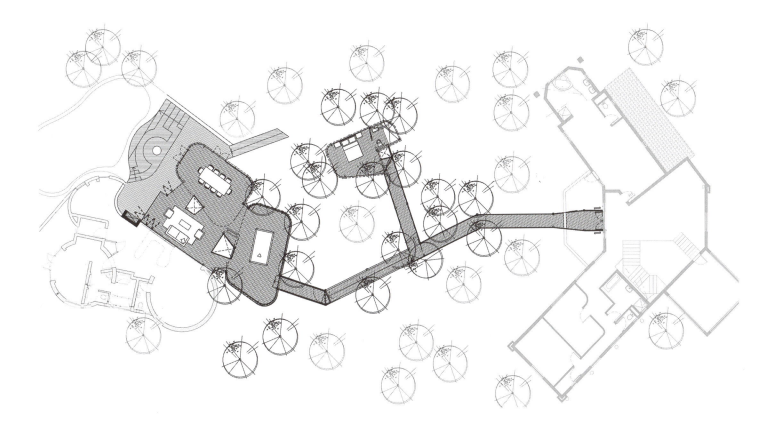

H

F Seating and dining seperated by a tree
G Bedroom glazed on three sides
H Floor plan
I Long table and full-hight glazing

136

FORMA ARCHITECTURE

ROCKY MOUNTAIN HOUSE #1

137 ROCKY MOUNTAIN HOUSE #1

CARBONDALE
CO, USA

AREA
190 m²

YEAR
2021

PHOTOGRAPHY
Dylan Brown

The Rocky Mountain House #1 is a four-bedroom, three-bathroom Nordic-style house situated on the outskirts of Carbondale, Colorado. The property is located on a creek frontage and features a bird sanctuary in the rear garden. This sustainable home offers a new way of living with smaller spaces and an emphasis on economic sustainability. It was designed with an independent rental unit to allow the owners to finance the property and expand it in the future should the family grow. The house was built to achieve a net zero standard, which includes continuous exterior insulation around the entire structure, thermal mass for the radiant floor, an electric water heat pump for hot water, an electric vehicle charger in the garage, large overhangs to the northwest to protect the large windows from direct sunlight, and other features.

A Front view of the house
B Living room
C Kitchen

138 FORMA ARCHITECTURE

D

E

D   Side view
E   View of the two terraces
F   Backside of the house
G   Garage entrance

139 ROCKY MOUNTAIN HOUSE #1

CARBONDALE
CO, USA

141 ROCKY MOUNTAIN HOUSE #1

CARBONDALE
CO, USA

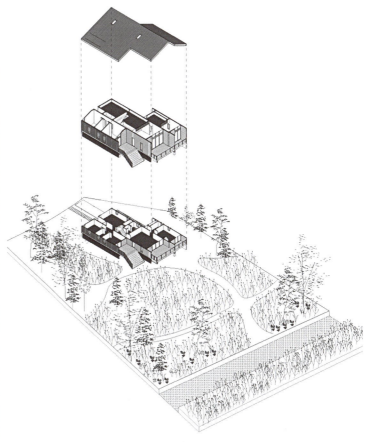

H Roof detail
I View from the window panel
J Living room
K Aerial view
L Component overview

|42

HOUSE K

ARCHITEKT TORSTEN HERRMANN

143 HOUSE K

ZIRL
AUSTRIA

AREA
177 m²

YEAR
2022

PHOTOGRAPHY
Gustav Willeit

The objective of this project was to create a home that strikes a balance between privacy and connection to nature. It was inspired by the concept of an indoor-outdoor space, as described by Sou Fujimoto. Centered around an inner courtyard, it facilitates a seamless transition from the exterior to the interior, effortlessly integrating nature into the living space. The first floor comprises the main living, dining, and cooking areas, which are open-plan, while the second floor contains the bedrooms and bathrooms, which are more private. The upper floor is framed to maintain privacy while directing views towards the inner courtyard. The white plastered frame has precisely positioned square openings of varying sizes, offering diverse views of the surrounding mountains. The building's exterior and interior feature a minimalist design with an emphasis on white elements.

A   Street view
B   Rear view of the house

ARCHITEKT TORSTEN HERRMANN

145 HOUSE K

ZIRL
AUSTRIA

C   View from the courtyard into the living area

ARCHITEKT TORSTEN HERRMANN

147 HOUSE K

ZIRL
AUSTRIA

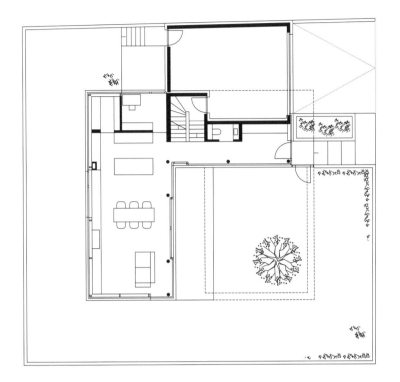
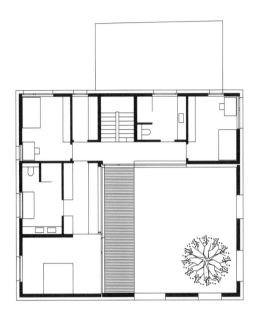

G H

D   View of the mountains from the courtyard
E   Dining area
F   Detail with the ruins of Fragenstein Castle
G   Ground floor plan
H   First floor plan

148

RIDGE 52 RESIDENCE

WARD | BLAKE ARCHITECTS

149 RIDGE 52 RESIDENCE

JACKSON
WY, USA

INTERIOR DESIGN
Ingrao, Inc.
LANDSCAPE DESIGN
Weaver & Associates
AREA
758.18 m²
YEAR
2019
PHOTOGRAPHY
Drew Orlando

This residence is on East Gros Ventre Butte, offering views of the surrounding mountains. It is integrated into the surrounding topography in a seamless manner, becoming an organic extension of the hillside. The underground garage has a sod roof that extends over the circulation areas of the plan and spans the length of the house. Low slope shed roofs extend beyond the house, safeguarding exterior spaces while ensuring optimal solar control for the interior. Incoporated into the design are stone walls and expansive glazing. The house is filled with natural light, warming the concrete below the floors. This provides comfort, stores energy, and offers daylight during the winter. The architectural style of the project evokes the rugged beauty of the region, while also incorporating a contemporary interpretation of the traditional Soddy Cabins that were constructed in late 19th-century frontier settlements.

A Twilight view from northwest
B View from the south looking towards the mountains

A

B

151 RIDGE 52 RESIDENCE

JACKSON
WY, USA

C   Living room with fireplace and mountain views

153 RIDGE 52 RESIDENCE

JACKSON WY, USA

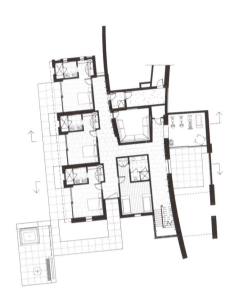
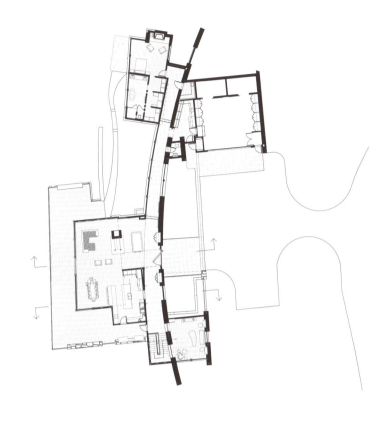

F G

D Living and dining room views
E Twilight view from west
F Lower floor plan
G Main floor plan
H Kitchen

H

154

AICHER ARCHITEKTEN

HOUSE IM REBGÄRTLE

155 HOUSE IM REBGÄRTLE

BREGENZ
AUSTRIA

AREA
237 m²

YEAR
2020

PHOTOGRAPHY
Bruno Klomfar
www.klomfar.com

The House im Rebgärtle, named after a former vineyard, is located on the slope of the Pfänder, the most famous mountain near Bregenz. The house, facing Lake Constance and the Rhine Valley, extends over three levels, with the top level containing the open-plan living area. The lower levels contain bedrooms and various other functional areas for the extended family. The entrance is on the lower floor. The building is characterized by cantilevered exposed concrete canopies, floor-to-ceiling wood-aluminum glazing with sliding doors and stone façades in between. The sliding slatted elements of the upper terrace provide additional sun and privacy protection. The sober exposed concrete façade to the north anchors the volume. An infinity pool and outdoor sauna below form a transverse wing to the main building and create a courtyard-like garden area protected from downdraughts.

A Southwest view, from the slope
B Northeast façade, the backbone of the building

157 HOUSE IM REBGÄRTLE

BREGENZ
AUSTRIA

C   Detail of the entrance on the buildings lower level
D   Southwest façade seen from the middle level

AICHER ARCHITEKTEN

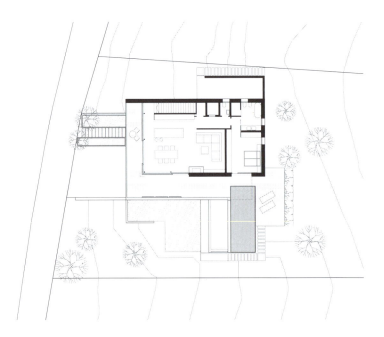

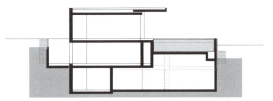

E   View from the living room over Lake Constance
F   Floor plan upper level with pool and section
G   View of the pool and mountain from the upper terrace
H   View west, from the access road

159 HOUSE IM REBGÄRTLE

BREGENZ
AUSTRIA

160 NO FOOTPRINT WOOD HOUSE

A-01 (A COMPANY / A FOUNDATION)

161 NO FOOTPRINT WOOD HOUSE

UVITA
COSTA RICA

AREA
450 m²

YEAR
2022

PHOTOGRAPHY
Fernando Alda
www.fernandoalda.com

The No Footprint Wood House is located along the southern Pacific coast of Costa Rica. Its bioclimatic design integrates with the surrounding natural habitat. The project forms part of the multi-award-winning No Footprint House (NFH) series. The modular NFH was developed in response to a roadmap for carbon neutrality in Costa Rica. Climate-responsive building variations are based on passive design strategies such as site-specific positioning and the use of natural resources. Industrial construction techniques are combined with renewable and locally sourced materials. The wooden house was built with a laminated teak wood system, a systemic kit of parts for sustainable construction. It was developed by the architects in collaboration with the national construction industry and international expertise.

A   Main facade
B   Mountain view
C   Spatial adaptation

A-01 (A COMPANY / A FOUNDATION)

163 NO FOOTPRINT WOOD HOUSE

UVITA
COSTA RICA

D Inside-out view to surrounding natural habitat

A-01 (A COMPANY / A FOUNDATION)

165 NO FOOTPRINT WOOD HOUSE

UVITA
COSTA RICA

G

H I

E   Main elevation open and closed
F   Floor plan
G   Private space
H   Terrace and pool
I   Cozy corner

166 O'CASELLA

ATELIER LAVIT

167 O'CASELLA

SARI-SOLENZARA
FRANCE

AREA
13 m²

YEAR
2022

PHOTOGRAPHY
Atelier LAVIT

O'Casella is a prefab modular wood cabin system with two distinct elements: the living module and the pergola. The living module offers space for technical areas like services and the kitchen, as well as a living and sleeping area with a view of the surrounding nature. The second volume, the pergola, is a shaded outdoor space for relaxing. An outdoor shower lets one enjoy the great outdoors. The wood used for the coverings and structure is local larch, which is durable and lightweight. Inside, the room has medium density fiberboard walls and a ceiling. As a distinctive sign, the façade has a steel rail that marks the horizontality of the entire volume. The track has a dual function: it gathers rainwater and guides the sliding façade shutter panel. This panel is a mashrabiya, a traditional windcatcher used for cooling, sun protection, and nighttime darkening. The prefab cabin can be transported on a truck.

A — Front view
B — Covered in wood

169 O'CASELLA

SARI-SOLENZARA
FRANCE

E F

C   Sliding façade shutter panel
    open
D   Sliding façade shutter panel
    closed
E   Outdoor shower
F   Living area
G   Entrance to pergola

G

171 O'CASELLA

SARI-SOLENZARA
FRANCE

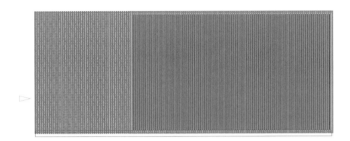
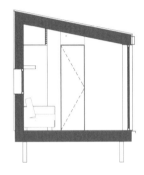
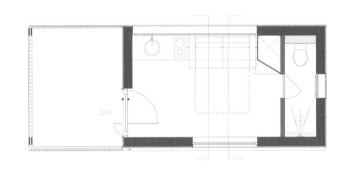
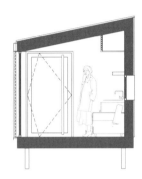

L   Plans

H   Pergola
I   Terrace
J   Mountain view
K   View from above
L   Plans

172

GANGOLY & KRISTINER ARCHITEKTEN

HOUSE BETWEEN THE MOUNTAINS

A

173 HOUSE BETWEEN THE MOUNTAINS

AUSSEERLAND
AUSTRIA

AREA
445 m²

YEAR
2017

PHOTOGRAPHY
David Schreyer
www.schreyerdavid.com

Building in Ausseerland is characterized by its typical traditional architecture, which is above all known for its respect for the landscape. Combining this special atmosphere with the idea of a timeless, comfortable house for family and guests was a challenge. The cross-shaped floor plan creates a link to regional models, defines the views of the lake and the mountains, and at the same time creates spatial zoning. The focus is on wood as cladding material. Externally it is used as a pre-grayed shell, while inside, in combination with exposed concrete and brass elements, it creates a warm atmosphere without a rustic echo. At the same time — and in combination with large areas of glazing against the backdrop of the breathtaking mountain scenery — the idea of combining transparency and security is successfully implemented.

A   North side with closed sliding panels
B   View of the TV room through the kitchen
C   Open fireplace with kitchen in the background

B C

GANGOLY & KRISTINER ARCHITEKTEN

175 HOUSE BETWEEN THE MOUNTAINS

AUSSEERLAND
AUSTRIA

D   View from the valley with mountain scenery

GANGOLY & KRISTINER ARCHITEKTEN

E

F

177 HOUSE BETWEEN THE MOUNTAINS

AUSSEERLAND
AUSTRIA

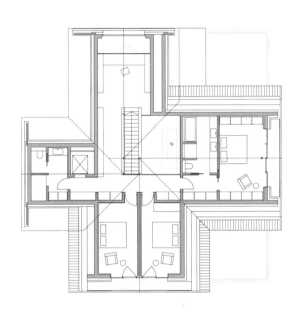

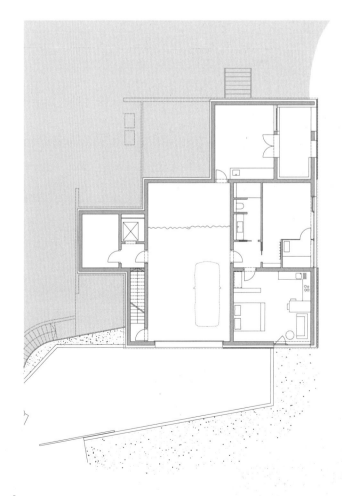

G H

E   Living room
F   Brass sliding door with velvet wall covering
G   Top floor plan
H   Ground floor plan
I   Basement floor plan

178

ABRAMSON ARCHITECTS

SAPIRE RESIDENCE

179 SAPIRE RESIDENCE

LOS ANGELES
CA, USA

AREA
1,580 m²

YEAR
2019

PHOTOGRAPHY
Erin Feinblatt

With a spectacular view of the Santa Monica Mountains and the Pacific Ocean, this hillside home opens to a fresh sea breeze and panoramic views. The stepped roof plan and informal layout offers the illusion of several smaller interconnected structures woven into the canyon rim. A minimal palette of natural materials is central to the design philosophy. Wide plank rustic oak flooring and oak shiplap walls and ceilings play off the weathered stone flooring and poured in place board-formed concrete walls. Wall panels and the kitchen cabinetry are clad in oil-rubbed bronze while the steel windows and exterior metals are painted to match. Motorized sliding doors of steel and glass frame views and allow for daylighting deep into the common spaces. When the doors are open, the house and patio are one spectacular space.

A   Vegetated hillside breaks up the volume on three sides
B   Materials indoor and outdoor match
C   Volumes merge into one another

ABRAMSON ARCHITECTS

181 SAPIRE RESIDENCE

LOS ANGELES
CA, USA

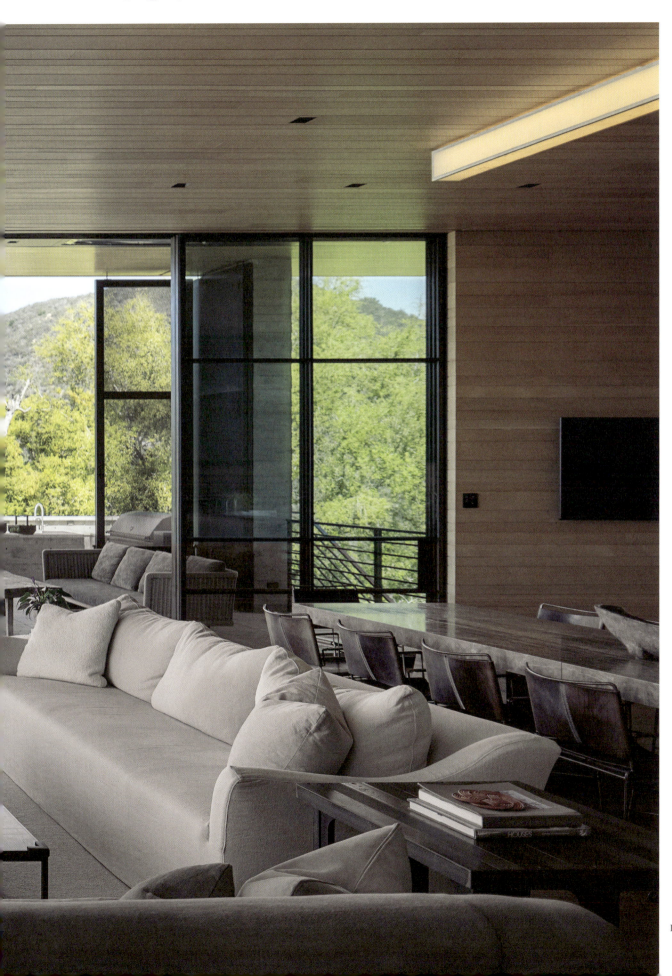

D Minimal palette of natural materials reflects the homeowners' passion for healthy living

182

ABRAMSON ARCHITECTS

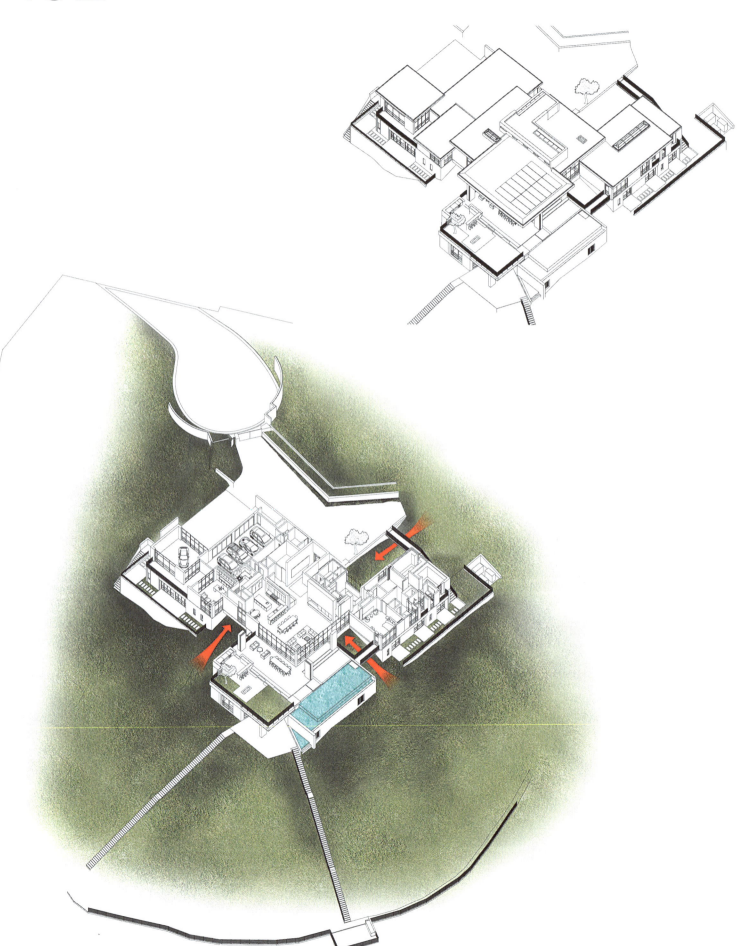

183 SAPIRE RESIDENCE

LOS ANGELES
CA, USA

F

G

H

E   Axonometry plans
F   House seems like single story development from below
G   Bronze tone of windows match oil-rubbed kitchen cabinets
H   Play of light and shadow by clerestory windows and skylights

184   LP ARCHITEKTUR

ZEIT. RAUM. WENG.

185 ZEIT. RAUM. WENG.

GOLDEGG
AUSTRIA

AREA
214 m²

YEAR
2019

PHOTOGRAPHY
Markus Rohrbacher

In Weng, a district of Goldegg, an aging farmhouse was replaced by a new three-story building that blends into the existing topography. Situated on a hillside, it was built with reinforced concrete and solid cross-laminated timber walls. A wooden staircase leads to the entrance level with a seminar area, a kitchen, and a practice room. Untreated spruce is used as the main material in the basement and on the upper floor. The building represents an ark farm that is intended to serve all people and animals as a space for learning or as a sheltered home and meeting place. Precisely placed openings create a dialogue between inside and outside, a connection to nature that makes it possible to consciously experience the course of the day and the year.

A Exterior view with surrounding mountains
B Front view

187 ZEIT. RAUM. WENG.

GOLDEGG
AUSTRIA

C   Panoramic view of the mountains

189 ZEIT. RAUM. WENG.

GOLDEGG
AUSTRIA

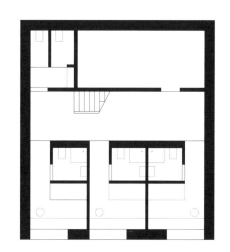
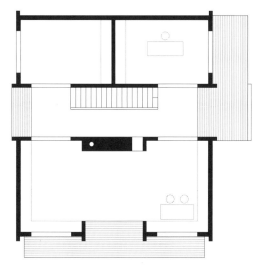
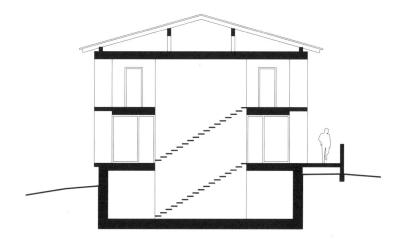

G

D   Living area
E   View through the corridor
F   Wooden stairs
G   Plans

190 CHALET D

LUPO & ZUCCARELLO ARCHITEKTEN

191

CHALET D

LINTHAL
SWITZERLAND

AREA
145 m²

YEAR
2018

PHOTOGRAPHY
Bruno Helbling
www.helblingfotografie.ch

In the Glarus Alps, this chalet that reinterprets traditional materials in a modern way has been built. The owner, a carpenter and mason, placed great emphasis on material selection: The spruce wood cladding was charred and brushed to create a natural patina, and the concrete is left raw and untreated. Supported by local craftsmen, he personally took on the construction and exposed concrete work. The house blends discreetly into the landscape, reminiscent of a typical hay barn. The panoramic window, which runs along three sides, visually separates the wooden structure from the concrete base, creating the impression that the building is floating. Clear lines, minimalist design, and precise craftsmanship characterize the interior. The close collaboration with architect Stefan Lupo resulted in a concept that meets both the strict building regulations for agricultural zones and the aesthetic aspirations of the project.

A   The idea of a hayloft on stilts
B   The modern kitchen
C   The integrated Fireplace

LUPO & ZUCCARELLO ARCHITEKTEN

193 CHALET D

LINTHAL
SWITZERLAND

D   Integrated into the surroundings

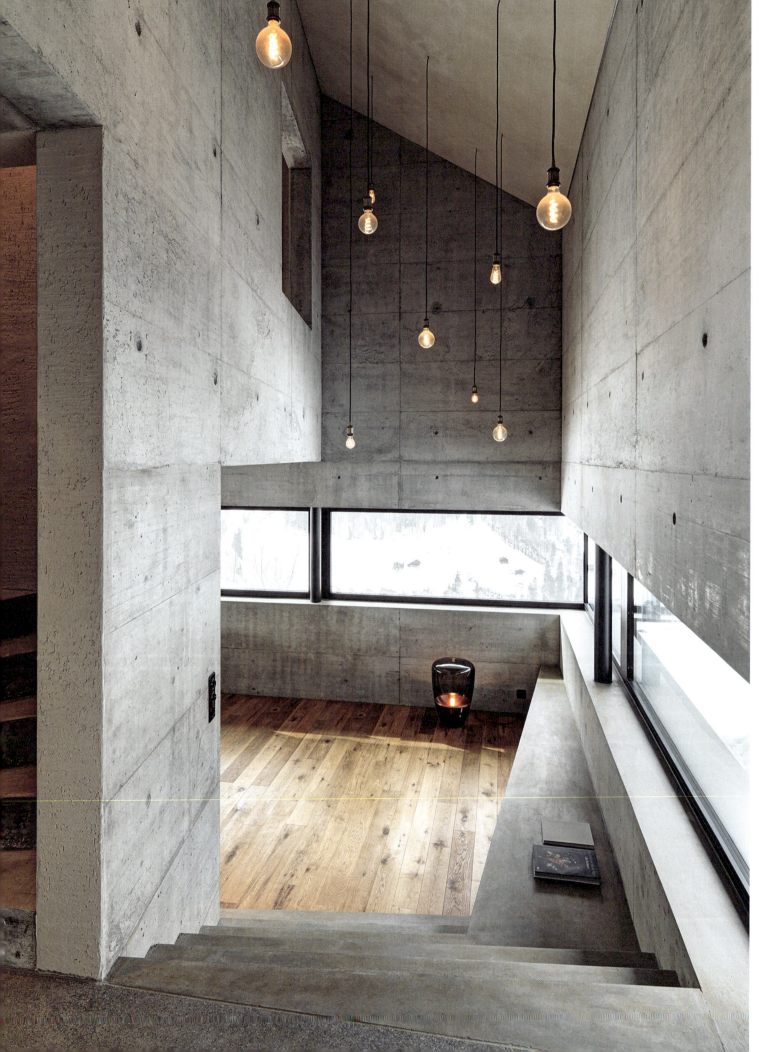

195 CHALET D

LINTHAL
SWITZERLAND

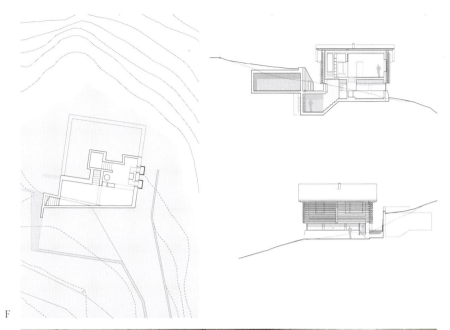

F

G

H

E   Panoramic window view
F   Floor plan
G   Open room concept
H   Passage between garage and residential building

196

CAREZZA
HOUSE

TARA

197 CAREZZA HOUSE

WELSCHNOFEN
ITALY

AREA
350 m²

YEAR
2021

PHOTOGRAPHY
Davide Perbellini
www.davideperbellini.com

This is a house in South Tyrol with many functions. It can serve as summer house, winter house, mountain house, and family home. In many ways, the Carezza House is a retreat, a place of longing, a place of well-being. The interlocking double pitched roof is the result of rotation and offset in height, creating interesting spatial situations both, inside and outside. In contrast to the exterior, which has a certain roughness due to the sometimes harsh weather conditions of the region, the interiors are refined. The materials used — wood, natural stone and steel — are brought to a high level of craftsmanship. This results in special rooms that make up this place of well-being, in which the senses open up and absorb everything that flows together in this house: mountain world, living culture, time for encounters, and appreciation.

A Front view
B Mountain view from the back

199 CAREZZA HOUSE

WELSCHNOFEN
ITALY

D

E

F

C   Stairs to the top floor
D   Living room and kitchen
E   Kitchen counter
F   Kitchen

201 CAREZZA HOUSE

WELSCHNOFEN
ITALY

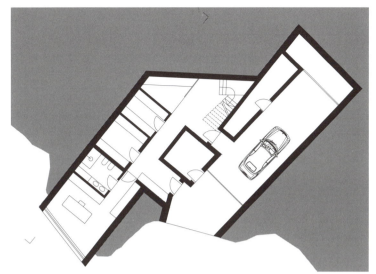
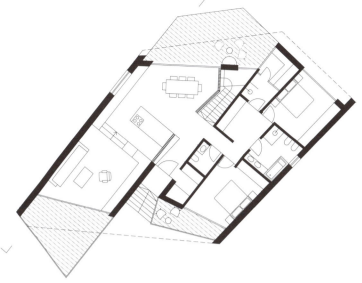
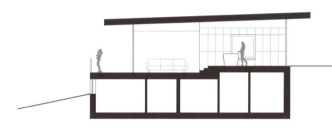

G   Back of the building
H   Front of the building
I   Floor plans and cross section
J   Cozy corner

202
MM HOUSE

BENJAMIN GOÑI ARQUITECTOS
CLARO + WESTENDARP ARQUITECTOS

203 MM HOUSE

LAGO RUPANCO
CHILE

AREA
473 m²

YEAR
2023

PHOTOGRAPHY
Nico Saieh
www.nicosaieh.cl

MM House is located on a hillside among native trees on the north shore of a lake in southern Chile. The design preserves all the trees and integrates views of the volcanoes, lake, and surrounding vegetation. The main challenge was dealing with the nearly 45-degree slope. The layout consists of two parallel bars that are aligned with the slope at different levels: The upper bar contains the master bedroom and living room, while the lower bar houses the children's bedrooms. These bars are connected by a larger volume for common spaces, including the kitchen, dining room, and terrace. To diminish heavy rainfall, the design incorporates simple volumes, using the roof over the lower bedroom as a covered terrace. The exterior features demolition larch shingles for low maintenance, while the interior features local pine siding.

A   Aerial view
B   View of the roofed terrace and the bedroom volume

BENJAMIN GOÑI ARQUITECTOS
CLARO + WESTENDARP ARQUITECTOS

205 MM HOUSE

LAGO RUPANCO
CHILE

C View of the main bedroom terrace

207 MM HOUSE

LAGO RUPANCO
CHILE

E

F G

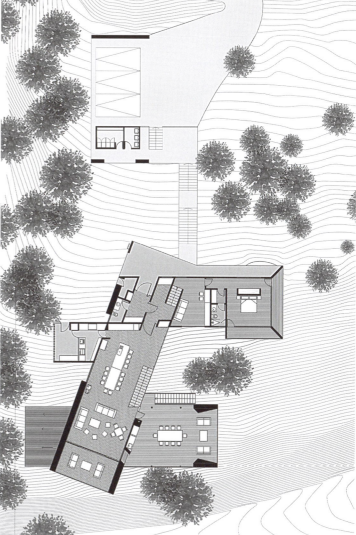

D Entry
E Exterior view of the house between the trees
F Living room
G Site plan and main story

208

THE THREE SUMMITS

NÓS ARCHITECTS

209 THE THREE SUMMITS

GREEN MOUNTAINS
VT, USA

AREA
951 m²

YEAR
2022

PHOTOGRAPHY
Eric Petschek (A,B, F–J),
Ryan Bent (C–E)

The Three Summits House is located at the highest point of the Green Mountains in Vermont, with stunning views of the valley. On the intermediate level, just below the main entrance, is a central pavilion. While the three-story pavilion contains a ground floor unit, two dormitories, and suites accessible from the garden level, the top pavilion is accessible directly from the garage and contains the master suite. Granite blocks frame the site and contain the interior spaces. Stone monoliths on the first floor form the base of the triangular prisms. The building is designed to unfold into the landscape, borrowing colors and textures from nature. The pavilions are connected by courtyards and strategically placed on the site to allow the whole to constantly evolve. It offers a variety of spaces to accommodate the different stages of human existence and is built to the highest standards, ensuring resilience and durability.

A   General view of the house
B   Aerial view toward mansfield mountain

NÓS ARCHITECTS

C   Open kitchen and living room
D   Master bedroom with cozy corner
E   View from the pool and main pavillion

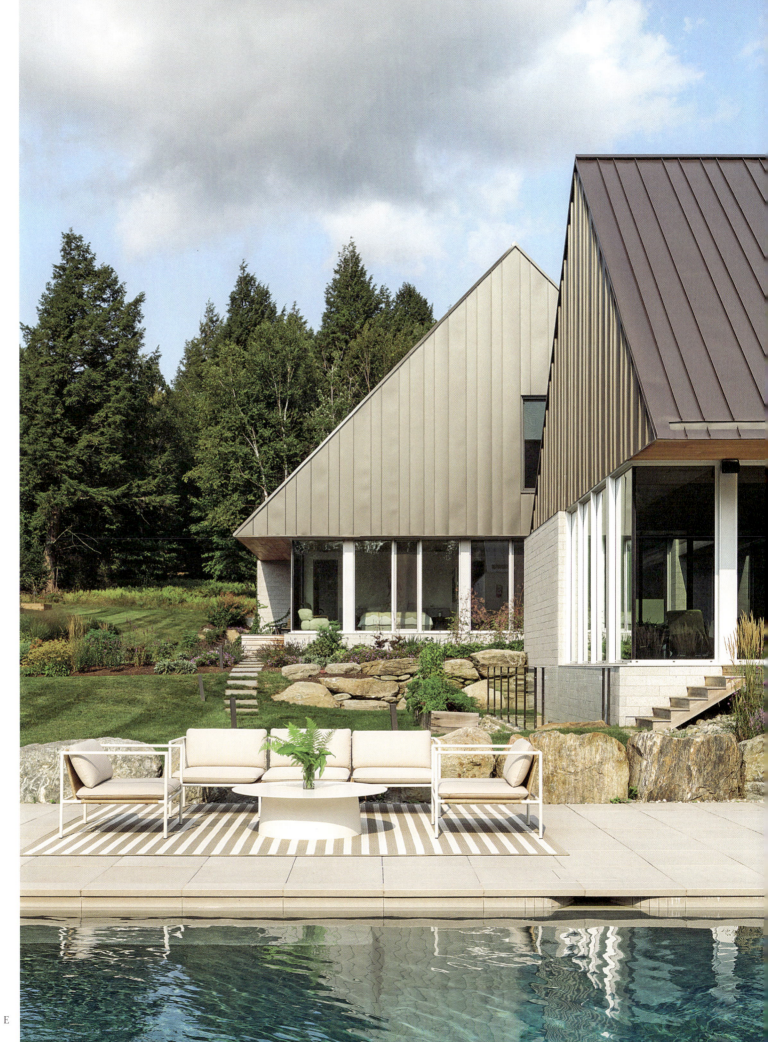

213 THE THREE SUMMITS

GREEN MOUNTAINS
VT, USA

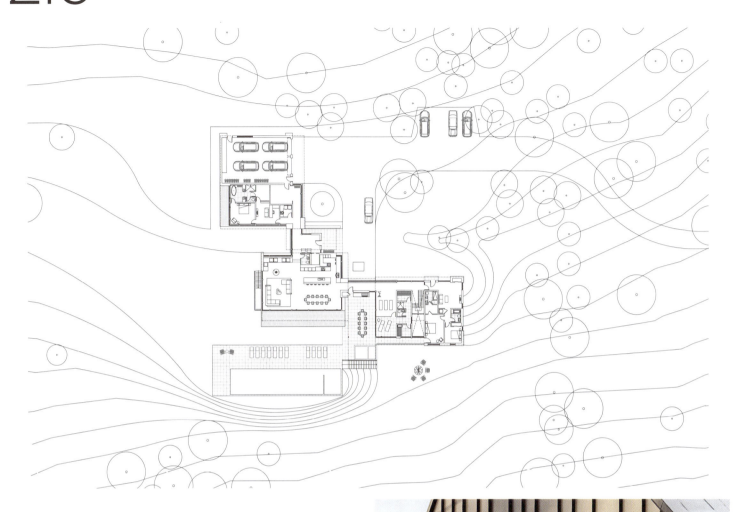

F   Roofs farming mountain peak
G   Detail of the three peaks
H   Main entry
I   Floor plan
J   Detail of metal cladding

2|4

EL MONTAÑES

GONZALO ITURRIAGA ARQUITECTOS

215 EL MONTAÑES

SAN ESTEBAN
CHILE

AREA
65 m²
YEAR
2023
PHOTOGRAPHY
Pablo Casals Aguirre

This residence occupies a prominent location on the slopes of Cerro del Cobre, offering sweeping views. It is positioned at a precise angle relative to the natural topography of the terrain. El Montañes is situated at a height that attempts to occupy a central position between as well as on the rocks that define the surrounding space. The project's space is enclosed by two concrete walls, which define the internal configuration of the structure. The façade has three elements: staircase and opening, mountain view, and compact enclosures. A modest terrace sits on the floor's sharpest corner. The elevated design overcomes the challenges of the rocky terrain, using local rock for 60 percent of the structure. Additionally, the perimeter coverings and closures are constructed from heat-treated wood and are sealed with primers. The glass façades are composed of an external glued thermopane system.

A   Outside view at dusk
B   Outside view at night

GONZALO ITURRIAGA ARQUITECTOS

217 EL MONTAÑES

SAN ESTEBAN
CHILE

C   Mountain views through living area

D

E F

219

EL MONTAÑES

SAN ESTEBAN
CHILE

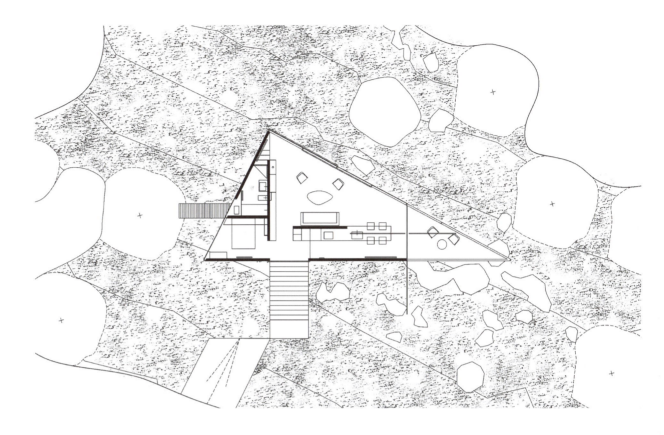

D Glass façade
E Living area
F Terrace views
G Ground floor plan
H Ladder

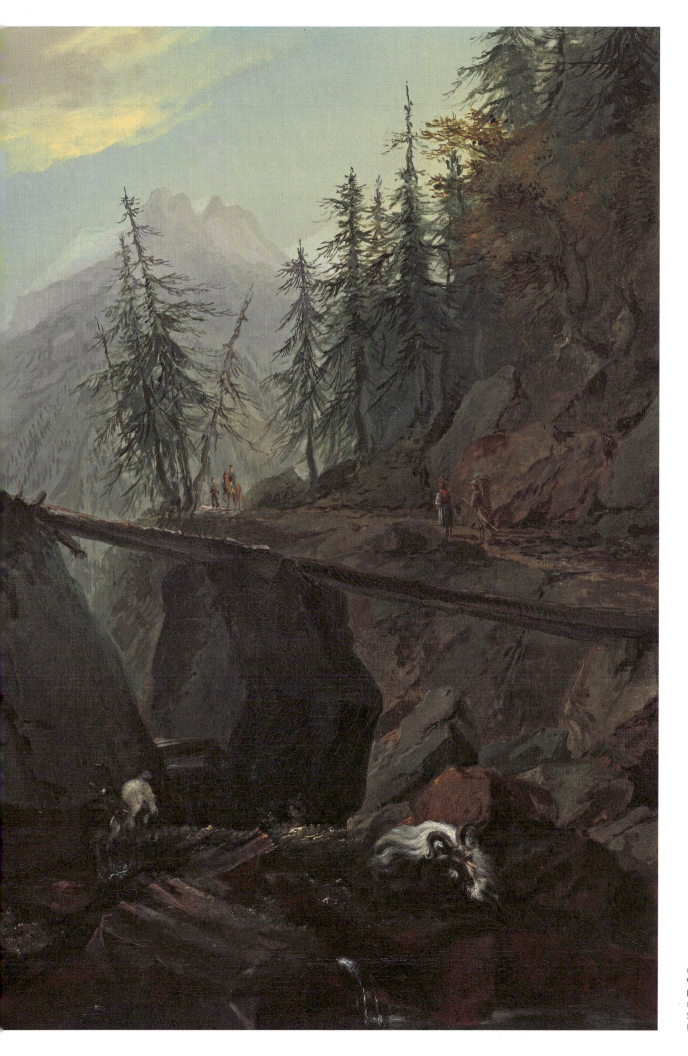

Caspar Goar Wolf
Wooden footbridge over the Lütschine near Gsteig, 1774
Oil/canvas
53, 5 cm × 81 cm
Kunstmuseum Winterthur, Switzerland

ARCHITECTS + STUDIOS

A

A-01 (A Company / A Foundation)
www.a-01.net
Photo Credits
Fernando Alda
www.fernandoalda.com
160–165

Abramson Architects
www.abramsonarchitects.com
Photo Credits
Erin Feinblatt
178–183

ADR
www.adr.cz
Photo Credits
BoysPlayNice
www.boysplaynice.com
22–27

Aicher Architekten
www.aicher-architekten.at
Photo Credits
Bruno Klomfar
www.klomfar.com
154–159

Architect Agustín Berzero
Photo Credits
Federico Cairoli
www.federicocairoli.com
28–33

Architekt Torsten Herrmann
www.torstenherrmann.com
Photo Credits
Gustav Willeit
142–147

Atelier Boom-Town
www.boom-town.ca
Photo Credits
Raphaël Thibodeau
52–57

Atelier Jörg Rügemer
www.ruegemer.com
Photo Credits
Paul Richer
www.richerimages.com
118–123

Atelier LAVIT
www.atelier-lavit.com
Photo Credits
Atelier LAVIT
166–171

B

BENJAMIN GOÑI ARQUITECTOS
www.bga.cl
Photo Credits
Nico Saieh
www.nicosaieh.cl
202–207

Blankpage Architects
www.blankpagearch.com
Photo Credits
Wissam Chaaya
www.wissamchaaya.com
88–93

Bogenfeld Architektur ZT GmbH
www.bogenfeld.at
Photo Credits
David Schreyer
www.schreyerdavid.com
70–75

C

Catharina Fineder Architektur
www.catharinafineder.com
Photo Credits
Petra Rainer
82–87

CLARO + WESTENDARP ARQUITECTOS
www.cwa.cl
Photo Credits
Nico Saieh
www.nicosaieh.cl
202–207

counson architectes
www.counson-architecte.ch
Photo Credits
Leo Fabrizio
112–117

cruu architecture
www.cruu.group
Photo Credits
Markus Mehwald
www.mehwald.net
76–81

D

Drawbox Design Studio Architects
www.drawboxstudio.co.za
Photo Credits
Natasha Dawjee Laurent
www.papercutphotography.com
130–135

F

Forma Architecture
www.formaarchitecture.com
Photo Credits
Dylan Brown
136–141

G

Gangoly & Kristiner Architekten
www.gangoly.at
Photo Credits
David Schreyer
www.schreyerdavid.com
172–177

Gonzalo Iturriaga Arquitectos
www.gonzaloiturriaga.cl
Photo Credits
Pablo Casals Aguirre
214–219

I

IDEE architects
www.idee.vn
Photo Credits
Triệu Chiến
16–21

K

Kündig & El Sadek GmbH
www.kundigelsadek.ch
Photo Credits
Kündig & El Sadek GmbH
106–111

ARCHITECTS + STUDIOS

L

Lepannen Anker Arquitectura
www.lepannenanker.com
Photo Credits
BICUBIK (A–C, E)
bicubik.photo
JAG STUDIO (D,F)
jagstudio.ec
34–39

LP architektur
www.lparchitektur.at
Photo Credits
Markus Rohrbacher
184–189

Lupo and Zuccarello Architekten AG SIA
www.lupozuccarello.ch
Photo Credits
Bruno Helbling
www.helblingfotografie.ch
190–195

M

Michael Welle Architektur
www.michael-welle.de
Photo Credits
Jürgen Pollak & Patrick Möhrle
124–129

monovolume architecture + design
www.monovolume.cc
Photo Credits
Giovanni De Sandre
www.giovannidesandre.com
10–15

Arch. D.I Martin Mostböck. AID. ArchitectureInteriorsDesign
www.martin-mostboeck.com
Photo Credits
Nathan Murrell
www.nathanmurrellphotos.com
100–105

N

N O S architects inc.
www.n-o-s.ca
Photo Credits
Eric Petschek (A,B, F–J)
Ryan Bent (C–E)
208–213

Mahesh Naik
www.architectmaheshnaik.com
Photo Credits
Mahesh Naik (A–C, F)
Omkar Jagdale and Musaib (E)
46–51

P

Pérez Palacios Arquitectos Asociados
www.ppaa.mx
Photo Credits
Rafael Gamo
www.rafaelgamo.com
58–63

R

Resolution: 4 Architecture
www.re4a.com
Photo Credits
Gavin Preuss/ Home and Property Photography LLC
www.homeandproperty-photography.com
64–69

S

SPIECKER SAUTTER LAUER ARCHITEKTEN
www.spsl.de
Photo Credits
Manfred Sautter (A, C)
Yohan Zerdoun (B, D–G)
www.yohanzerdoun.com
94–99

Studio d'architettura Concerpio
www.studioconceprio.ch
Photo Credits
Giacomo Albo
www.finearc.it
40–45

T

tara- Arch. Heike Pohl, Arch. Andreas Zanier
www.arch-tara.it
Photo Credits
Davide Perbellini
www.davideperbellini.com
196–201

Tectum Arquitectura Architect Manuel Gonzalez Veglia
www.tectumarq.com
Photo Credits
Federico Cairoli
www.federicocairoli.com
28–33

W

Ward | Blake Architects
www.wardblake.com
Photo Credits
Drew Orlando
148–153

Wespi de Meuron Romeo architects
www.wdmra.ch
Photo Credits
Giacomo Albo
www.finearc.it
40–45

IMPRINT

The Deutsche Nationalbibliothek lists this publication in the Deutsche Nationalbibliografie; detailed bibliographic data are available on the Internet at http://dnb.dnb.de.

ISBN 978-3-03768-303-3

© 2025 by Braun Publishing AG

www.braun-publishing.ch

The work is copyright protected. Any use outside of the close boundaries of the copyright law, which has not been granted permission by the publisher, is unauthorized and liable for prosecution. This especially applies to duplications, translations, microfilming, and any saving or processing in electronic systems.

1st edition 2025

Editor
Editorial Office van Uffelen

Editorial staff and layout
Elmedina Kolgeci, Chris van Uffelen

Graphic concept
Eva Finkbeiner

Reproduction
BildIDruck GmbH, Berlin

All of the information in this volume has been compiled to the best of the editor's knowledge. It is based on the information provided to the publisher by the architects' and designers' offices and excludes any liability. The publisher assumes no responsibility for its accuracy or completeness as well as copyright discrepancies and refers to the specified sources (architects' and designers' offices). All rights to the photographs are property of the photographer (please refer to the pages and the index).

Product Safety
Publisher: Braun Publishing AG, Arenenbergstr. 2, 8268 Salenstein, Switzerland, publisher@braun-publishing.ch
EU-Representative: Bookwise GmbH, Zeppelinstr. 67, 81669 Munich, Germany, info@bookwise.de